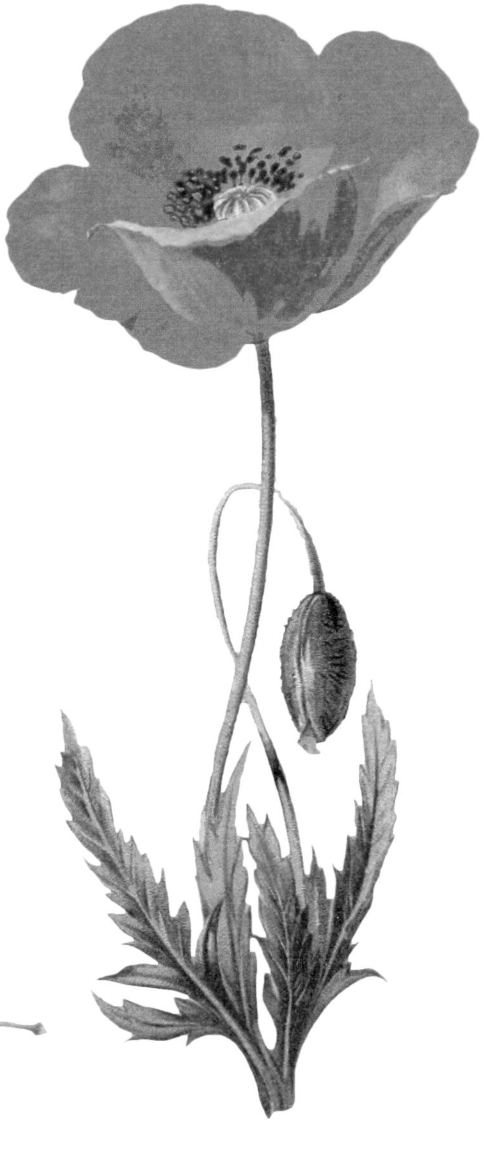

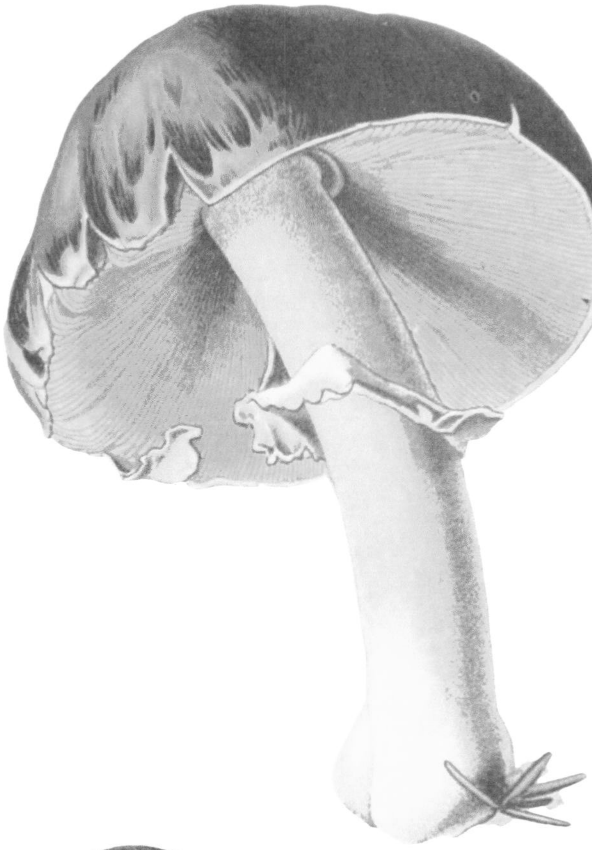

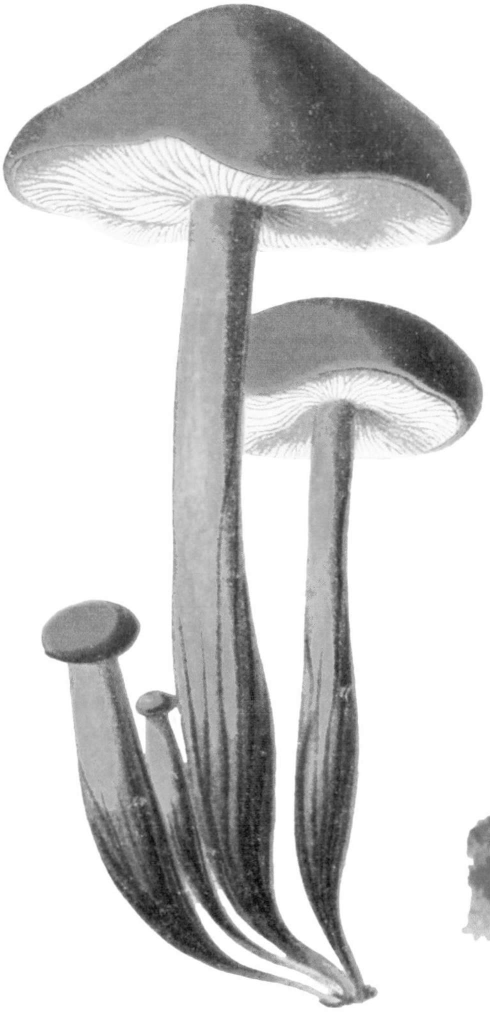

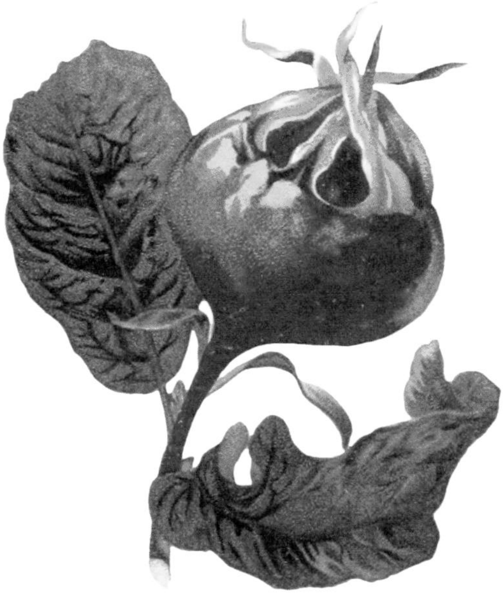

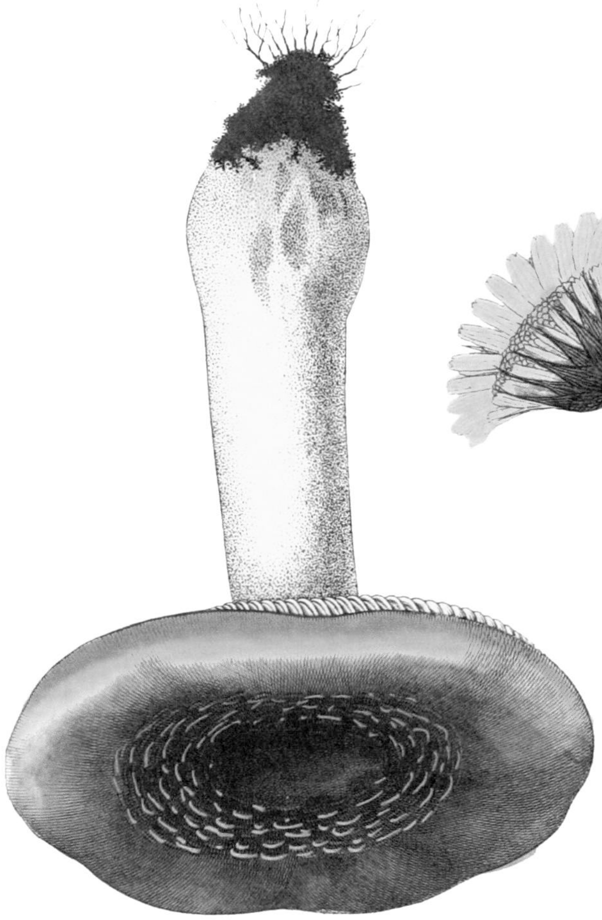

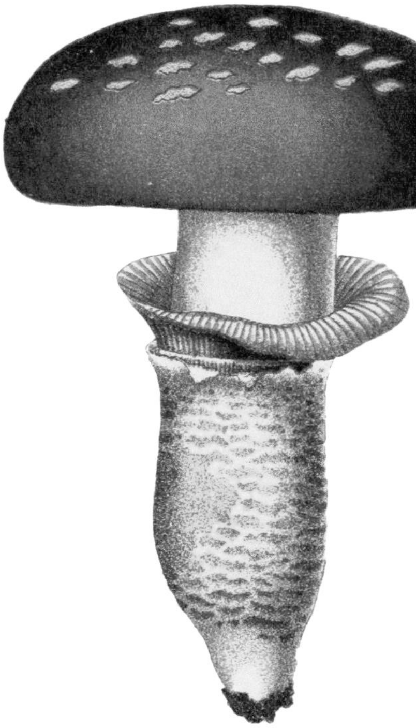

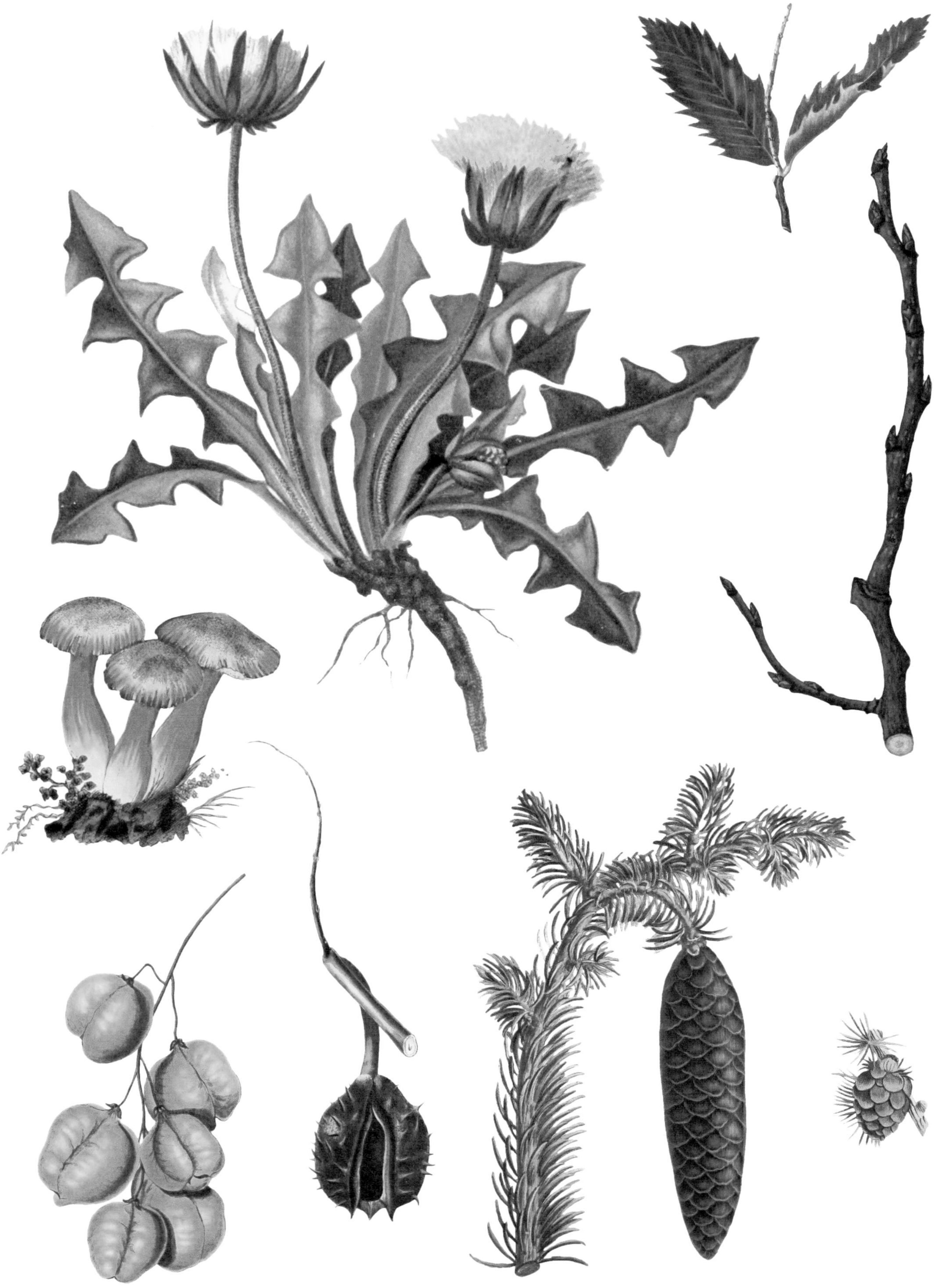

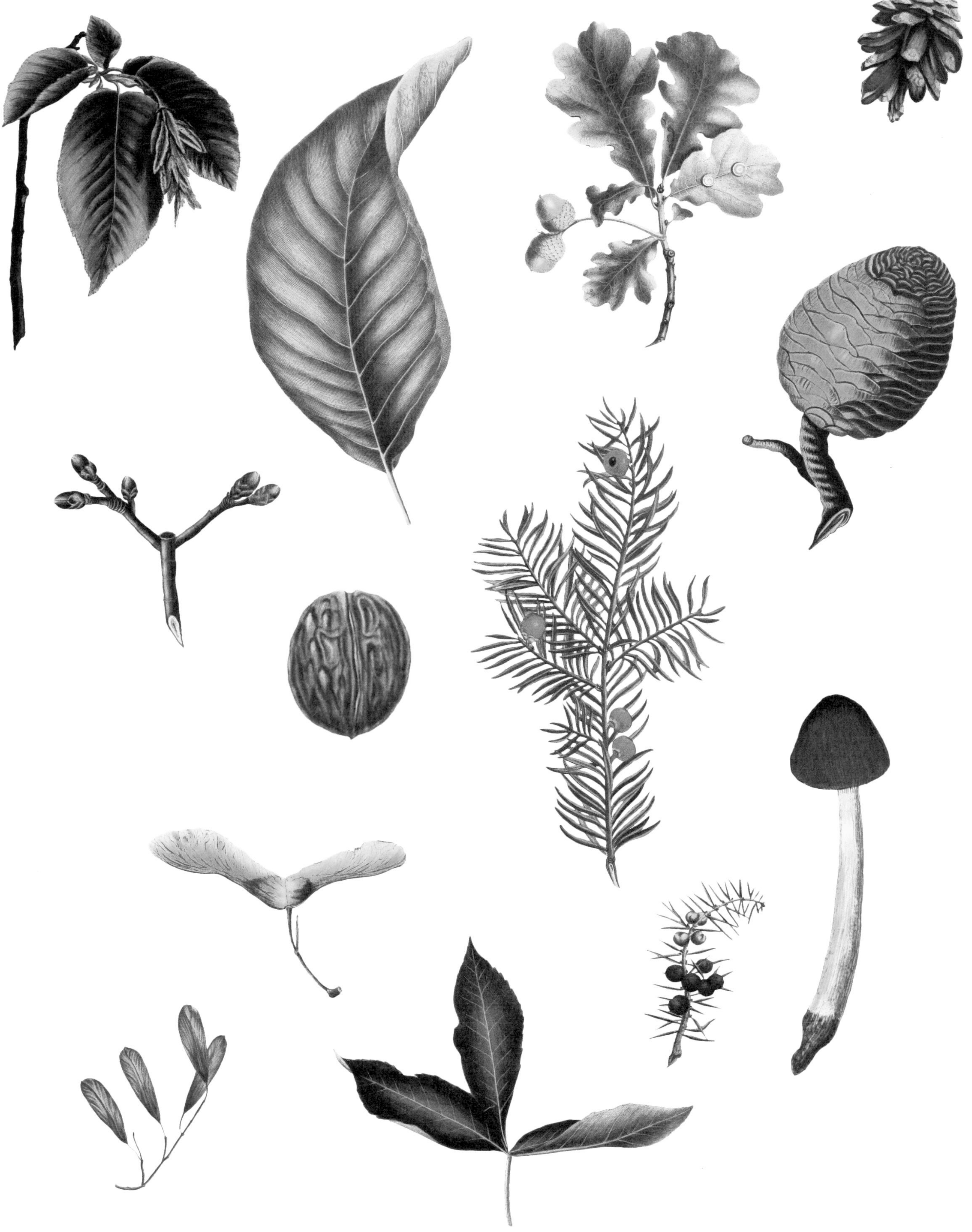

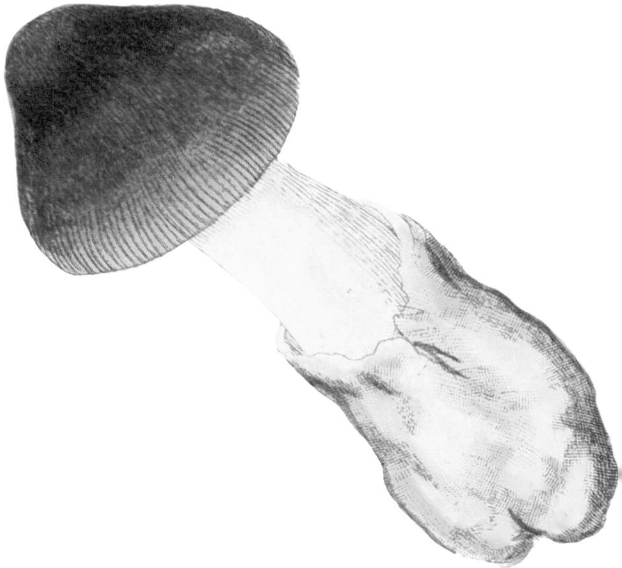

I’d love to hear your honest opinion

★★★★★

Made in United States
Troutdale, OR
04/06/2025

30359822R00043